PROGRESS NOTES FOR SPECIAL NEEDS KIDS

ITSOKALLY.COM

INDEX

CHILD'S NAME: YEAR:

USE THIS PAGE AS A QUICK GUIDE TO KNOW WHICH COLOURED SECTION OF THE BOOK HOLDS THE CORRESPONDING NOTES FOR THE GOALS YOU ARE WORKING ON.

DOING THIS SAVES FLIPPING PAGES BACK AND FORTH EACH TIME YOU WANT TO WRITE YOUR NOTES

WRITE YOUR CHILD'S GOAL BELOW	FIND YOUR NOTES FOR EACH GOAL IN THE COLOURED SECTION LISTED
	AQUA
	ORANGE
	PURPLE
	PINK
	AQUA
	ORANGE
	PURPLE
	PINK

PROGRESS NOTES FOR SPECIAL NEEDS KIDS

Hi! I'm Ally's mum and wanted to say hi, and thank you for your purchase from itsokally.com

The workbook you are using today, is a real product made to support Ally, myself, and our support network, in achieving Ally's yearly goals, and is designed to be used in the following way.

 +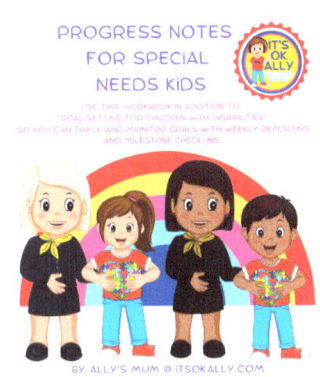

With the help of your support team or family, choose the most important goals you want to work on achieving from the Goal Setting Book for Children with Disabilities, and then transfer those goals over into this new book, either as a photocopy, or by re-writing them again.

At the start of each new coloured section in the book, there is a place for you to do this. You'll notice there are 8 x different coloured sections, for 8 x different goals your child is working on each year.

The different coloured sections help you distinguish between each goal you are working on quickly and easily, and there is also an index at the front of the book for easy reference that will tell you what goals belong to what colour too!

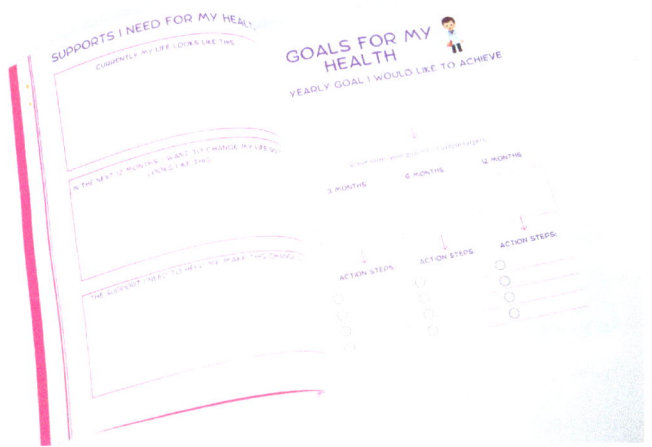

PROGRESS NOTES FOR SPECIAL NEEDS KIDS

Next, you'll notice that there are spaces for weekly note taking or reporting from week #1, up to week #52 with milestone check-in's at 3 months, 6 months, and 12 months.

Use these placeholders to write weekly summaries on the progress your child is making in achieving their goals, and when it's time to write your milestones, be sure to list your child's achievements, no matter how big or small.

If you have trouble finding time to write your notes in the book yourself, or it becomes too overwhelming for you (which is what happens to me!) consider reaching out to a trusted person in your support network to help you. This may be a support worker, partner, teacher, allied health professional, or even another parent or friend. Your support group is there to help, so be sure to let them know what you need, so they can support you in the way that is best :)

If you have any feedback or comments on using your book, feel free to reach out and say hello. You can usually find me at: itsokally.com

Much love

Ally's Mum xo

ITSOKALLY.COM

PROGRESS NOTES FOR SPECIAL NEEDS KIDS

ITSOKALLY.COM

SUPPORTS I NEED TO HELP ME REACH MY GOAL

CURRENTLY MY LIFE LOOKS LIKE THIS:

IN THE NEXT 12 MONTHS I WANT TO CHANGE MY LIFE SO IT LOOKS LIKE THIS:

THE SUPPORT I NEED TO HELP ME MAKE THIS CHANGE IS:

YEARLY GOAL

YEARLY GOAL I WOULD LIKE TO ACHIEVE

BREAK DOWN YOUR GOAL INTO 3 SIMPLE TARGETS:

3 MONTHS	6 MONTHS	12 MONTHS

ACTION STEPS:
- ○ _____
- ○ _____
- ○ _____
- ○ _____

ACTION STEPS:
- ○ _____
- ○ _____
- ○ _____
- ○ _____

ACTION STEPS:
- ○ _____
- ○ _____
- ○ _____
- ○ _____

GOAL TRACKER

WEEK #1

Notes

WEEK #2

Notes

WEEK #3

Notes

WEEK #4

Notes

GOAL TRACKER

WEEK #5

Notes

WEEK #6

Notes

WEEK #7

Notes

WEEK #8

Notes

GOAL TRACKER

WEEK #9

Notes

WEEK #10

Notes

WEEK #11

Notes

WEEK #12

Notes

YEARLY GOAL

YEARLY GOAL I WOULD LIKE TO ACHIEVE

BREAK DOWN YOUR GOAL INTO 3 SIMPLE TARGETS:

3 MONTHS	6 MONTHS	12 MONTHS

ACTION STEPS: ACTION STEPS: ACTION STEPS:

- ○
- ○
- ○
- ○

GOAL TRACKER

WEEK #1

Notes

WEEK #2

Notes

WEEK #3

Notes

WEEK #4

Notes

GOAL TRACKER

WEEK #5
Notes

WEEK #6
Notes

WEEK #7
Notes

WEEK #8
Notes

GOAL TRACKER

WEEK #9

Notes

WEEK #10

Notes

WEEK #11

Notes

WEEK #12

Notes

3 MONTH MILESTONE CHECK IN

ACHIEVEMENTS

- ○ _____
- ○ _____
- ○ _____
- ○ _____
- ○ _____
- ○ _____
- ○ _____
- ○ _____

ORIGINAL 3 MONTH MILESTONE GOAL

6 MONTH MILESTONE GOAL

NOTES

GOAL TRACKER

WEEK #13

Notes

WEEK #14

Notes

WEEK #15

Notes

WEEK #16

Notes

GOAL TRACKER

WEEK #17

Notes

WEEK #18

Notes

WEEK #19

Notes

WEEK #20

Notes

GOAL TRACKER

WEEK #21

Notes

WEEK #22

Notes

WEEK #23

Notes

WEEK #24

Notes

6 MONTH MILESTONE CHECK IN

ACHIEVEMENTS

- ○ _____
- ○ _____
- ○ _____
- ○ _____
- ○ _____
- ○ _____
- ○ _____
- ○ _____

ORIGINAL 6 MONTH MILESTONE GOAL

12 MONTH MILESTONE GOAL

NOTES

GOAL TRACKER

WEEK #25

Notes

WEEK #26

Notes

WEEK #27

Notes

WEEK #28

Notes

GOAL TRACKER

WEEK #29

Notes

WEEK #30

Notes

WEEK #31

Notes

WEEK #32

Notes

GOAL TRACKER

WEEK #33

Notes

WEEK #34

Notes

WEEK #35

Notes

WEEK #36

Notes

GOAL TRACKER

WEEK #37
Notes

WEEK #38
Notes

WEEK #39
Notes

WEEK #40
Notes

GOAL TRACKER

WEEK #41

Notes

WEEK #42

Notes

WEEK #43

Notes

WEEK #44

Notes

GOAL TRACKER

WEEK #45

Notes

WEEK #46

Notes

WEEK #47

Notes

WEEK #48

Notes

GOAL TRACKER

WEEK #49
Notes

WEEK #50
Notes

WEEK #51
Notes

WEEK #52
Notes

12 MONTH MILESTONE CHECK IN

ACHIEVEMENTS

- ○ _____
- ○ _____
- ○ _____
- ○ _____
- ○ _____
- ○ _____
- ○ _____
- ○ _____

ORIGINAL 12 MONTH MILESTONE GOAL

SUMMARY OF ACHIEVEMENT FOR 12 MONTHS

NOTES

GOAL TRACKER

SUMMARY #1

Notes

SUMMARY #2

Notes

SUMMARY #3

Notes

SUMMARY #4

Notes

PROGRESS NOTES FOR SPECIAL NEEDS KIDS

ITSOKALLY.COM

SUPPORTS I NEED TO HELP ME REACH MY GOAL

CURRENTLY MY LIFE LOOKS LIKE THIS:

IN THE NEXT 12 MONTHS I WANT TO CHANGE MY LIFE SO IT LOOKS LIKE THIS:

THE SUPPORT I NEED TO HELP ME MAKE THIS CHANGE IS:

YEARLY GOAL

YEARLY GOAL I WOULD LIKE TO ACHIEVE

BREAK DOWN YOUR GOAL INTO 3 SIMPLE TARGETS:

3 MONTHS	6 MONTHS	12 MONTHS

ACTION STEPS:
- ○ _____
- ○ _____
- ○ _____
- ○ _____

ACTION STEPS:
- ○ _____
- ○ _____
- ○ _____
- ○ _____

ACTION STEPS:
- ○ _____
- ○ _____
- ○ _____
- ○ _____

GOAL TRACKER

WEEK #1

Notes

WEEK #2

Notes

WEEK #3

Notes

WEEK #4

Notes

GOAL TRACKER

WEEK #5

Notes

WEEK #6

Notes

WEEK #7

Notes

WEEK #8

Notes

GOAL TRACKER

WEEK #9

Notes

WEEK #10

Notes

WEEK #11

Notes

WEEK #12

Notes

3 MONTH MILESTONE CHECK IN

ACHIEVEMENTS

- ○ _____
- ○ _____
- ○ _____
- ○ _____
- ○ _____
- ○ _____
- ○ _____
- ○ _____

ORIGINAL 3 MONTH MILESTONE GOAL

6 MONTH MILESTONE GOAL

NOTES

GOAL TRACKER

WEEK #13

Notes

WEEK #14

Notes

WEEK #15

Notes

WEEK #16

Notes

GOAL TRACKER

WEEK #17
Notes

WEEK #18
Notes

WEEK #19
Notes

WEEK #20
Notes

GOAL TRACKER

WEEK #21

Notes

WEEK #22

Notes

WEEK #23

Notes

WEEK #24

Notes

6 MONTH MILESTONE CHECK IN

ACHIEVEMENTS

- _____
- _____
- _____
- _____
- _____
- _____
- _____
- _____

ORIGINAL 6 MONTH MILESTONE GOAL

12 MONTH MILESTONE GOAL

NOTES

GOAL TRACKER

WEEK #25

Notes

WEEK #26

Notes

WEEK #27

Notes

WEEK #28

Notes

GOAL TRACKER

WEEK #29

Notes

WEEK #30

Notes

WEEK #31

Notes

WEEK #32

Notes

GOAL TRACKER

WEEK #33

Notes

WEEK #34

Notes

WEEK #35

Notes

WEEK #36

Notes

GOAL TRACKER

WEEK #37

Notes

WEEK #38

Notes

WEEK #39

Notes

WEEK #40

Notes

GOAL TRACKER

WEEK #41

Notes

WEEK #42

Notes

WEEK #43

Notes

WEEK #44

Notes

GOAL TRACKER

WEEK #45

Notes

WEEK #46

Notes

WEEK #47

Notes

WEEK #48

Notes

GOAL TRACKER

WEEK #49

Notes

WEEK #50

Notes

WEEK #51

Notes

WEEK #52

Notes

12 MONTH MILESTONE CHECK IN

ACHIEVEMENTS

- ○ _____
- ○ _____
- ○ _____
- ○ _____
- ○ _____
- ○ _____
- ○ _____
- ○ _____

ORIGINAL 12 MONTH MILESTONE GOAL

SUMMARY OF ACHIEVEMENT FOR 12 MONTHS

NOTES

GOAL TRACKER

SUMMARY #1

Notes

SUMMARY #2

Notes

SUMMARY #3

Notes

SUMMARY #4

Notes

PROGRESS NOTES FOR SPECIAL NEEDS KIDS

ITSOKALLY.COM

SUPPORTS I NEED TO HELP ME REACH MY GOAL

CURRENTLY MY LIFE LOOKS LIKE THIS:

IN THE NEXT 12 MONTHS I WANT TO CHANGE MY LIFE SO IT LOOKS LIKE THIS:

THE SUPPORT I NEED TO HELP ME MAKE THIS CHANGE IS:

YEARLY GOAL

YEARLY GOAL I WOULD LIKE TO ACHIEVE

BREAK DOWN YOUR GOAL INTO 3 SIMPLE TARGETS:

3 MONTHS	6 MONTHS	12 MONTHS

ACTION STEPS:
- ○ _____
- ○ _____
- ○ _____
- ○ _____

ACTION STEPS:
- ○ _____
- ○ _____
- ○ _____
- ○ _____

ACTION STEPS:
- ○ _____
- ○ _____
- ○ _____
- ○ _____

GOAL TRACKER

WEEK #1

Notes

WEEK #2

Notes

WEEK #3

Notes

WEEK #4

Notes

GOAL TRACKER

WEEK #5

Notes

WEEK #6

Notes

WEEK #7

Notes

WEEK #8

Notes

GOAL TRACKER

WEEK #9

Notes

WEEK #10

Notes

WEEK #11

Notes

WEEK #12

Notes

3 MONTH MILESTONE CHECK IN

ACHIEVEMENTS

- ○ _____
- ○ _____
- ○ _____
- ○ _____
- ○ _____
- ○ _____
- ○ _____
- ○ _____

ORIGINAL 3 MONTH MILESTONE GOAL

6 MONTH MILESTONE GOAL

NOTES

GOAL TRACKER

WEEK #13

Notes

WEEK #14

Notes

WEEK #15

Notes

WEEK #16

Notes

GOAL TRACKER

WEEK #17
Notes

WEEK #18
Notes

WEEK #19
Notes

WEEK #20
Notes

GOAL TRACKER

WEEK #21

Notes

WEEK #22

Notes

WEEK #23

Notes

WEEK #24

Notes

6 MONTH MILESTONE CHECK IN

ACHIEVEMENTS

- ○ _____
- ○ _____
- ○ _____
- ○ _____
- ○ _____
- ○ _____
- ○ _____
- ○ _____

ORIGINAL 6 MONTH MILESTONE GOAL

12 MONTH MILESTONE GOAL

NOTES

GOAL TRACKER

WEEK #25

Notes

WEEK #26

Notes

WEEK #27

Notes

WEEK #28

Notes

GOAL TRACKER

WEEK #29
Notes

WEEK #30
Notes

WEEK #31
Notes

WEEK #32
Notes

GOAL TRACKER

WEEK #33

Notes

WEEK #34

Notes

WEEK #35

Notes

WEEK #36

Notes

GOAL TRACKER

WEEK #37

Notes

WEEK #38

Notes

WEEK #39

Notes

WEEK #40

Notes

GOAL TRACKER

WEEK #41

Notes

WEEK #42

Notes

WEEK #43

Notes

WEEK #44

Notes

GOAL TRACKER

WEEK #45
Notes

WEEK #46
Notes

WEEK #47
Notes

WEEK #48
Notes

GOAL TRACKER

WEEK #49

Notes

WEEK #50

Notes

WEEK #51

Notes

WEEK #52

Notes

12 MONTH MILESTONE CHECK IN

ACHIEVEMENTS

- ○ _____
- ○ _____
- ○ _____
- ○ _____
- ○ _____
- ○ _____
- ○ _____
- ○ _____

ORIGINAL 12 MONTH MILESTONE GOAL

SUMMARY OF ACHIEVEMENT FOR 12 MONTHS

NOTES

GOAL TRACKER

SUMMARY #1

Notes

SUMMARY #2

Notes

SUMMARY #3

Notes

SUMMARY #4

Notes

PROGRESS NOTES FOR SPECIAL NEEDS KIDS

ITSOKALLY.COM

SUPPORTS I NEED TO HELP ME REACH MY GOAL

CURRENTLY MY LIFE LOOKS LIKE THIS:

IN THE NEXT 12 MONTHS I WANT TO CHANGE MY LIFE SO IT LOOKS LIKE THIS:

THE SUPPORT I NEED TO HELP ME MAKE THIS CHANGE IS:

YEARLY GOAL

YEARLY GOAL I WOULD LIKE TO ACHIEVE

BREAK DOWN YOUR GOAL INTO 3 SIMPLE TARGETS:

3 MONTHS	6 MONTHS	12 MONTHS

ACTION STEPS: ACTION STEPS: ACTION STEPS:

- ○
- ○
- ○
- ○

GOAL TRACKER

WEEK #1

Notes

WEEK #2

Notes

WEEK #3

Notes

WEEK #4

Notes

GOAL TRACKER

WEEK #5
Notes

WEEK #6
Notes

WEEK #7
Notes

WEEK #8
Notes

GOAL TRACKER

WEEK #9

Notes

WEEK #10

Notes

WEEK #11

Notes

WEEK #12

Notes

YEARLY GOAL

YEARLY GOAL I WOULD LIKE TO ACHIEVE

BREAK DOWN YOUR GOAL INTO 3 SIMPLE TARGETS:

3 MONTHS	6 MONTHS	12 MONTHS

ACTION STEPS: **ACTION STEPS:**   **ACTION STEPS:**

GOAL TRACKER

WEEK #1

Notes

WEEK #2

Notes

WEEK #3

Notes

WEEK #4

Notes

3 MONTH MILESTONE CHECK IN

ACHIEVEMENTS

- ○ _____
- ○ _____
- ○ _____
- ○ _____
- ○ _____
- ○ _____
- ○ _____
- ○ _____

ORIGINAL 3 MONTH MILESTONE GOAL

6 MONTH MILESTONE GOAL

NOTES

GOAL TRACKER

WEEK #13

Notes

WEEK #14

Notes

WEEK #15

Notes

WEEK #16

Notes

GOAL TRACKER

WEEK #17

Notes

WEEK #18

Notes

WEEK #19

Notes

WEEK #20

Notes

GOAL TRACKER

WEEK #21

Notes

WEEK #22

Notes

WEEK #23

Notes

WEEK #24

Notes

6 MONTH MILESTONE CHECK IN

ACHIEVEMENTS

○ _____
○ _____
○ _____
○ _____
○ _____
○ _____
○ _____
○ _____

ORIGINAL 6 MONTH MILESTONE GOAL

12 MONTH MILESTONE GOAL

NOTES

GOAL TRACKER

WEEK #25

Notes

WEEK #26

Notes

WEEK #27

Notes

WEEK #28

Notes

GOAL TRACKER

WEEK #29

Notes

WEEK #30

Notes

WEEK #31

Notes

WEEK #32

Notes

GOAL TRACKER

WEEK #33

Notes

WEEK #34

Notes

WEEK #35

Notes

WEEK #36

Notes

GOAL TRACKER

WEEK #37

Notes

WEEK #38

Notes

WEEK #39

Notes

WEEK #40

Notes

GOAL TRACKER

WEEK #41

Notes

WEEK #42

Notes

WEEK #43

Notes

WEEK #44

Notes

GOAL TRACKER

WEEK #45

Notes

WEEK #46

Notes

WEEK #47

Notes

WEEK #48

Notes

GOAL TRACKER

WEEK #49

Notes

WEEK #50

Notes

WEEK #51

Notes

WEEK #52

Notes

12 MONTH MILESTONE CHECK IN

ACHIEVEMENTS

- ○ _____
- ○ _____
- ○ _____
- ○ _____
- ○ _____
- ○ _____
- ○ _____
- ○ _____

ORIGINAL 12 MONTH MILESTONE GOAL

SUMMARY OF ACHIEVEMENT FOR 12 MONTHS

NOTES

_____
_____
_____
_____
_____
_____

GOAL TRACKER

SUMMARY #1

Notes

SUMMARY #2

Notes

SUMMARY #3

Notes

SUMMARY #4

Notes

PROGRESS NOTES FOR SPECIAL NEEDS KIDS

ITSOKALLY.COM

SUPPORTS I NEED TO HELP ME REACH MY GOAL

CURRENTLY MY LIFE LOOKS LIKE THIS:

IN THE NEXT 12 MONTHS I WANT TO CHANGE MY LIFE SO IT LOOKS LIKE THIS:

THE SUPPORT I NEED TO HELP ME MAKE THIS CHANGE IS:

YEARLY GOAL

YEARLY GOAL I WOULD LIKE TO ACHIEVE

BREAK DOWN YOUR GOAL INTO 3 SIMPLE TARGETS:

3 MONTHS	6 MONTHS	12 MONTHS

ACTION STEPS:
- ○ _____
- ○ _____
- ○ _____
- ○ _____

ACTION STEPS:
- ○ _____
- ○ _____
- ○ _____
- ○ _____

ACTION STEPS:
- ○ _____
- ○ _____
- ○ _____
- ○ _____

GOAL TRACKER

WEEK #1

Notes

WEEK #2

Notes

WEEK #3

Notes

WEEK #4

Notes

GOAL TRACKER

WEEK #5

Notes

WEEK #6

Notes

WEEK #7

Notes

WEEK #8

Notes

GOAL TRACKER

WEEK #9

Notes

WEEK #10

Notes

WEEK #11

Notes

WEEK #12

Notes

3 MONTH MILESTONE CHECK IN

ACHIEVEMENTS

- ○ _____
- ○ _____
- ○ _____
- ○ _____
- ○ _____
- ○ _____
- ○ _____
- ○ _____

ORIGINAL 3 MONTH MILESTONE GOAL

6 MONTH MILESTONE GOAL

NOTES

GOAL TRACKER

WEEK #13

Notes

WEEK #14

Notes

WEEK #15

Notes

WEEK #16

Notes

GOAL TRACKER

WEEK #17

Notes

WEEK #18

Notes

WEEK #19

Notes

WEEK #20

Notes

GOAL TRACKER

WEEK #21

Notes

WEEK #22

Notes

WEEK #23

Notes

WEEK #24

Notes

6 MONTH MILESTONE CHECK IN

ACHIEVEMENTS

- ○ _____
- ○ _____
- ○ _____
- ○ _____
- ○ _____
- ○ _____
- ○ _____
- ○ _____

ORIGINAL 6 MONTH MILESTONE GOAL

12 MONTH MILESTONE GOAL

NOTES

GOAL TRACKER

WEEK #25

Notes

WEEK #26

Notes

WEEK #27

Notes

WEEK #28

Notes

GOAL TRACKER

WEEK #29

Notes

WEEK #30

Notes

WEEK #31

Notes

WEEK #32

Notes

GOAL TRACKER

WEEK #33

Notes

WEEK #34

Notes

WEEK #35

Notes

WEEK #36

Notes

GOAL TRACKER

WEEK #37

Notes

WEEK #38

Notes

WEEK #39

Notes

WEEK #40

Notes

GOAL TRACKER

WEEK #41

Notes

WEEK #42

Notes

WEEK #43

Notes

WEEK #44

Notes

GOAL TRACKER

WEEK #45

Notes

WEEK #46

Notes

WEEK #47

Notes

WEEK #48

Notes

GOAL TRACKER

WEEK #49

Notes

WEEK #50

Notes

WEEK #51

Notes

WEEK #52

Notes

12 MONTH MILESTONE CHECK IN

ACHIEVEMENTS

- ○ _____
- ○ _____
- ○ _____
- ○ _____
- ○ _____
- ○ _____
- ○ _____
- ○ _____

ORIGINAL 12 MONTH MILESTONE GOAL

SUMMARY OF ACHIEVEMENT FOR 12 MONTHS

NOTES

GOAL TRACKER

SUMMARY #1

Notes

SUMMARY #2

Notes

SUMMARY #3

Notes

SUMMARY #4

Notes

PROGRESS NOTES FOR SPECIAL NEEDS KIDS

ITSOKALLY.COM

SUPPORTS i NEED TO HELP ME REACH MY GOAL

CURRENTLY MY LIFE LOOKS LIKE THIS:

IN THE NEXT 12 MONTHS I WANT TO CHANGE MY LIFE SO IT LOOKS LIKE THIS:

THE SUPPORT I NEED TO HELP ME MAKE THIS CHANGE IS:

YEARLY GOAL

YEARLY GOAL I WOULD LIKE TO ACHIEVE

BREAK DOWN YOUR GOAL INTO 3 SIMPLE TARGETS:

3 MONTHS	6 MONTHS	12 MONTHS

ACTION STEPS: ACTION STEPS: ACTION STEPS:

- ○ _____
- ○ _____
- ○ _____
- ○ _____

GOAL TRACKER

WEEK #1

Notes

WEEK #2

Notes

WEEK #3

Notes

WEEK #4

Notes

GOAL TRACKER

WEEK #5

Notes

WEEK #6

Notes

WEEK #7

Notes

WEEK #8

Notes

GOAL TRACKER

WEEK #9

Notes

WEEK #10

Notes

WEEK #11

Notes

WEEK #12

Notes

3 MONTH MILESTONE CHECK IN

ACHIEVEMENTS

- ○ _____
- ○ _____
- ○ _____
- ○ _____
- ○ _____
- ○ _____
- ○ _____
- ○ _____

ORIGINAL 3 MONTH MILESTONE GOAL

6 MONTH MILESTONE GOAL

NOTES

GOAL TRACKER

WEEK #13

Notes

WEEK #14

Notes

WEEK #15

Notes

WEEK #16

Notes

GOAL TRACKER

WEEK #17

Notes

WEEK #18

Notes

WEEK #19

Notes

WEEK #20

Notes

GOAL TRACKER

WEEK #21

Notes

WEEK #22

Notes

WEEK #23

Notes

WEEK #24

Notes

6 MONTH MILESTONE CHECK IN

ACHIEVEMENTS

- ○ _____
- ○ _____
- ○ _____
- ○ _____
- ○ _____
- ○ _____
- ○ _____
- ○ _____

ORIGINAL 6 MONTH MILESTONE GOAL

12 MONTH MILESTONE GOAL

NOTES

GOAL TRACKER

WEEK #25

Notes

WEEK #26

Notes

WEEK #27

Notes

WEEK #28

Notes

GOAL TRACKER

WEEK #29

Notes

WEEK #30

Notes

WEEK #31

Notes

WEEK #32

Notes

GOAL TRACKER

WEEK #33

Notes

WEEK #34

Notes

WEEK #35

Notes

WEEK #36

Notes

GOAL TRACKER

WEEK #37

Notes

WEEK #38

Notes

WEEK #39

Notes

WEEK #40

Notes

GOAL TRACKER

WEEK #41

Notes

WEEK #42

Notes

WEEK #43

Notes

WEEK #44

Notes

GOAL TRACKER

WEEK #45

Notes

WEEK #46

Notes

WEEK #47

Notes

WEEK #48

Notes

GOAL TRACKER

WEEK #49

Notes

WEEK #50

Notes

WEEK #51

Notes

WEEK #52

Notes

12 MONTH MILESTONE CHECK IN

ACHIEVEMENTS

- ○ _____
- ○ _____
- ○ _____
- ○ _____
- ○ _____
- ○ _____
- ○ _____
- ○ _____

ORIGINAL 12 MONTH MILESTONE GOAL

SUMMARY OF ACHIEVEMENT FOR 12 MONTHS

NOTES

GOAL TRACKER

SUMMARY #1

Notes

SUMMARY #2

Notes

SUMMARY #3

Notes

SUMMARY #4

Notes

PROGRESS NOTES FOR SPECIAL NEEDS KIDS

ITSOKALLY.COM

SUPPORTS I NEED TO HELP ME REACH MY GOAL

CURRENTLY MY LIFE LOOKS LIKE THIS:

IN THE NEXT 12 MONTHS I WANT TO CHANGE MY LIFE SO IT LOOKS LIKE THIS:

THE SUPPORT I NEED TO HELP ME MAKE THIS CHANGE IS:

YEARLY GOAL

YEARLY GOAL I WOULD LIKE TO ACHIEVE

BREAK DOWN YOUR GOAL INTO 3 SIMPLE TARGETS:

3 MONTHS	6 MONTHS	12 MONTHS

ACTION STEPS:
- ○ _____
- ○ _____
- ○ _____
- ○ _____

ACTION STEPS:
- ○ _____
- ○ _____
- ○ _____
- ○ _____

ACTION STEPS:
- ○ _____
- ○ _____
- ○ _____
- ○ _____

GOAL TRACKER

WEEK #1
Notes

WEEK #2
Notes

WEEK #3
Notes

WEEK #4
Notes

GOAL TRACKER

WEEK #5

Notes

WEEK #6

Notes

WEEK #7

Notes

WEEK #8

Notes

GOAL TRACKER

WEEK #9

Notes

WEEK #10

Notes

WEEK #11

Notes

WEEK #12

Notes

3 MONTH MILESTONE CHECK IN

ACHIEVEMENTS

- _____
- _____
- _____
- _____
- _____
- _____
- _____
- _____

ORIGINAL 3 MONTH MILESTONE GOAL

6 MONTH MILESTONE GOAL

NOTES

_____
_____
_____
_____
_____
_____

GOAL TRACKER

WEEK #13

Notes

WEEK #14

Notes

WEEK #15

Notes

WEEK #16

Notes

GOAL TRACKER

WEEK #17

Notes

WEEK #18

Notes

WEEK #19

Notes

WEEK #20

Notes

GOAL TRACKER

WEEK #21

Notes

WEEK #22

Notes

WEEK #23

Notes

WEEK #24

Notes

6 MONTH MILESTONE CHECK IN

ACHIEVEMENTS

- _____
- _____
- _____
- _____
- _____
- _____
- _____
- _____

ORIGINAL 6 MONTH MILESTONE GOAL

12 MONTH MILESTONE GOAL

NOTES

_____
_____
_____
_____
_____
_____

GOAL TRACKER

WEEK #25

Notes

WEEK #26

Notes

WEEK #27

Notes

WEEK #28

Notes

GOAL TRACKER

WEEK #29

Notes

WEEK #30

Notes

WEEK #31

Notes

WEEK #32

Notes

GOAL TRACKER

WEEK #33

Notes

WEEK #34

Notes

WEEK #35

Notes

WEEK #36

Notes

GOAL TRACKER

WEEK #37
Notes

WEEK #38
Notes

WEEK #39
Notes

WEEK #40
Notes

GOAL TRACKER

WEEK #41
Notes

WEEK #42
Notes

WEEK #43
Notes

WEEK #44
Notes

GOAL TRACKER

WEEK #45

Notes

WEEK #46

Notes

WEEK #47

Notes

WEEK #48

Notes

GOAL TRACKER

WEEK #49

Notes

WEEK #50

Notes

WEEK #51

Notes

WEEK #52

Notes

12 MONTH MILESTONE CHECK IN

ACHIEVEMENTS

- ○ _____
- ○ _____
- ○ _____
- ○ _____
- ○ _____
- ○ _____
- ○ _____
- ○ _____

ORIGINAL 12 MONTH MILESTONE GOAL

SUMMARY OF ACHIEVEMENT FOR 12 MONTHS

NOTES

GOAL TRACKER

SUMMARY #1

Notes

SUMMARY #2

Notes

SUMMARY #3

Notes

SUMMARY #4

Notes

PROGRESS NOTES FOR SPECIAL NEEDS KIDS

ITSOKALLY.COM

SUPPORTS I NEED TO HELP ME REACH MY GOAL

CURRENTLY MY LIFE LOOKS LIKE THIS:

IN THE NEXT 12 MONTHS I WANT TO CHANGE MY LIFE SO IT LOOKS LIKE THIS:

THE SUPPORT I NEED TO HELP ME MAKE THIS CHANGE IS:

YEARLY GOAL

YEARLY GOAL I WOULD LIKE TO ACHIEVE

BREAK DOWN YOUR GOAL INTO 3 SIMPLE TARGETS:

3 MONTHS	6 MONTHS	12 MONTHS

ACTION STEPS:
- ○ ___
- ○ ___
- ○ ___
- ○ ___

ACTION STEPS:
- ○ ___
- ○ ___
- ○ ___
- ○ ___

ACTION STEPS:
- ○ ___
- ○ ___
- ○ ___
- ○ ___

GOAL TRACKER

WEEK #1

Notes

WEEK #2

Notes

WEEK #3

Notes

WEEK #4

Notes

GOAL TRACKER

WEEK #5

Notes

WEEK #6

Notes

WEEK #7

Notes

WEEK #8

Notes

GOAL TRACKER

WEEK #9

Notes

WEEK #10

Notes

WEEK #11

Notes

WEEK #12

Notes

3 MONTH MILESTONE CHECK IN

ACHIEVEMENTS

- ○ _____
- ○ _____
- ○ _____
- ○ _____
- ○ _____
- ○ _____
- ○ _____
- ○ _____

ORIGINAL 3 MONTH MILESTONE GOAL

6 MONTH MILESTONE GOAL

NOTES

_____
_____
_____
_____
_____
_____

GOAL TRACKER

WEEK #13

Notes

WEEK #14

Notes

WEEK #15

Notes

WEEK #16

Notes

GOAL TRACKER

WEEK #17

Notes

WEEK #18

Notes

WEEK #19

Notes

WEEK #20

Notes

GOAL TRACKER

WEEK #21

Notes

WEEK #22

Notes

WEEK #23

Notes

WEEK #24

Notes

6 MONTH MILESTONE CHECK IN

ACHIEVEMENTS

- ○ _____
- ○ _____
- ○ _____
- ○ _____
- ○ _____
- ○ _____
- ○ _____
- ○ _____

ORIGINAL 6 MONTH MILESTONE GOAL

12 MONTH MILESTONE GOAL

NOTES

GOAL TRACKER

WEEK #25

Notes

WEEK #26

Notes

WEEK #27

Notes

WEEK #28

Notes

GOAL TRACKER

WEEK #29

Notes

WEEK #30

Notes

WEEK #31

Notes

WEEK #32

Notes

GOAL TRACKER

WEEK #33

Notes

WEEK #34

Notes

WEEK #35

Notes

WEEK #36

Notes

GOAL TRACKER

WEEK #37
Notes

WEEK #38
Notes

WEEK #39
Notes

WEEK #40
Notes

GOAL TRACKER

WEEK #41

Notes

WEEK #42

Notes

WEEK #43

Notes

WEEK #44

Notes

GOAL TRACKER

WEEK #45

Notes

WEEK #46

Notes

WEEK #47

Notes

WEEK #48

Notes

GOAL TRACKER

WEEK #49

Notes

WEEK #50

Notes

WEEK #51

Notes

WEEK #52

Notes

12 MONTH MILESTONE CHECK IN

ACHIEVEMENTS

- ○ _____
- ○ _____
- ○ _____
- ○ _____
- ○ _____
- ○ _____
- ○ _____
- ○ _____

ORIGINAL 12 MONTH MILESTONE GOAL

SUMMARY OF ACHIEVEMENT FOR 12 MONTHS

NOTES

GOAL TRACKER

SUMMARY #1

Notes

SUMMARY #2

Notes

SUMMARY #3

Notes

SUMMARY #4

Notes

itsokally.com is made with love
with help from
Mothers and Marketers

Mothers and Marketers invest
in purpose built products
for kids, teens and adults.

To learn more, or start a project of your
own, go to mothersandmarketers.com

www.ingramcontent.com/pod-product-compliance
Lightning Source LLC
Chambersburg PA
CBHW041158290426
44109CB00002B/54